Boston Celtics

Michael E. Goodman

CREATIVE ✿ EDUCATION

Published by Creative Education
123 South Broad Street, Mankato, Minnesota 56001
Creative Education is an imprint of The Creative Company

Designed by Rita Marshall

Photos by: Allsport Photography, Associated Press/Wide World Photos,
Focus on Sports, NBA Photos, UPI/Corbis-Bettmann, and SportsChrome.

Photo page 1: Larry Bird
Photo title page: Eric Williams

Library of Congress Cataloging-in-Publication Data

Goodman, Michael E.
Boston Celtics / Michael E. Goodman.
p. cm. — (NBA today)
Summary: Highlights the history and key players and coaches of the Boston
Celtics.
ISBN 0-88682-867-8

1. Boston Celtics (Basketball team)—History—Juvenile literature.
[1. Boston Celtics (Basketball team)—History. 2. Basketball—History.]
I. Title. II. Series: NBA today (Mankato, Minn.)

GV885.52.B67G66 1997   96-53184
796.32'364'0974461—dc21

First edition

5 4 3

American writer and philosopher Ralph Waldo Emerson once called Boston "the town which was appointed to lead the civilization of North America." Indeed, the citizens of Boston, Massachusetts, are very proud of their city's history and culture. Boston is the birthplace of freedom in the United States. It was founded in 1620 by a group of Puritans who crossed the Atlantic Ocean to escape religious and political persecution. A century and a half later, Bostonians fought the first battles of the American Revolution.

The pride and courage of Boston's past can still be felt in

1920: The pre-NBA Celtics.

Walter Brown drafted Charles Cooper, the first black player selected by an NBA team.

the spirit of the modern-day city. This is especially true where the Boston Celtics are concerned. The team is the most successful franchise in the history of professional basketball. The Celtics own 16 banners, one for each National Basketball Association (NBA) championship that the team has captured. What is the secret to Boston's success? Fans and players explain it in two words: "Celtic Pride."

"You never had to tell any member of the Celtics to dive for a loose ball or to play all out," said Hall of Famer John Havlicek, who starred in Boston Garden for 16 seasons. "We did those things without being asked or reminded. We had pride. That's the meaning of the Celtics."

Building the legend of the Boston Celtics over the years have been such players as Havlicek, Bob Cousy, Bill Russell, Sam Jones, K.C. Jones, Dave Cowens, Larry Bird, Kevin McHale, Robert Parish, Dennis Johnson, and many others. But what has made Celtics teams so special is not the individual greatness of the players, but their ability to blend into tight, hard-working units. "Victory belongs to the team, not the individual," long-time Celtics coach Red Auerbach used to tell his players.

Stars have come and gone over the years, and while Celtics teams were at or near the top of the league for many of those years, the 1990s have brought transition to the franchise. The hopes of the club now lie on the shoulders of Dino Radja, Antoine Walker, and new coach Rick Pitino. But with Celtic Pride strong as ever, fans hope the new Celtics will become as good as the teams of the past, bringing Boston's winning tradition into the next century.

Part of the Celtics legend, Robert Parish.

1 9 5 1

Ed Macauley was Boston's first All-Star and went on to average 18.9 points per game.

The Boston Celtics weren't always a winning team. During the club's first four seasons (1946–1950), it finished near the bottom of its division each year. Boston owner Walter Brown knew that something had to be done to turn his team around. He decided to start at the top, with a new coach. The man he chose was Arnold "Red" Auerbach.

The short and stocky Auerbach had a special fire inside him—an overwhelming desire to be the best—that he used to inspire his players to reach the tops of their games. "Everyone is born with a certain potential," he said, explaining his theory of life and sports. "You may never achieve your full potential, but how close you come depends on how much you want to pay the price. Many, many times, the kids with less talent become the better athletes because they're more dedicated to achieving their full potential."

Auerbach drove his players hard to help them reach their potential, especially during practice sessions. "If I so much as saw a player eating too much, I'd get on his case," he said. "I'd run him when he wanted to rest. If a guy loafed, I'd send him home and bring in somebody else. Discipline was always my byword. There were no chairs and no water allowed in practice. I demanded respect." That respect was translated on the court into pride, discipline, confidence, and victories.

Auerbach also spent more time working on defense than did most of his fellow coaches. "That was my style. I was always looking for the extra edge, and what better edge could you get than to have the man you were guarding lose his composure because you were putting a little extra pressure on him," Auerbach said.

When Auerbach arrived in Boston to begin planning for the 1950–51 season, the team that greeted him was a ragtag group of mediocre players. He felt the club needed size and experience, but fans in the Boston area had other ideas. They had their hopes pinned on a local college star named Bob Cousy, and they wanted Auerbach to choose him during that year's college draft. Though Cousy was only 6-foot-1, he had speed, great ballhandling ability, and a good scoring touch. And he desperately wanted to play for the Celtics in Boston.

Gene Conley served as a pitcher for the Braves and a reserve forward for the Celtics.

Cousy and the Boston fans were disappointed when Auerbach declined to pick the local star, but then a series of unusual events occurred. The NBA team in Chicago went out of business, and its players were distributed to other teams in the league. The Tri-Cities squad wanted to sign one of Chicago's best players, but could do so only if it gave up its first draft pick—Cousy. So Cousy's name was put into a hat along with those of two Chicago players. The Celtics would get to sign one of those players. Boston owner Walter Brown reached into the hat and chose the slip of paper with Cousy's name on it. It seemed that Bob Cousy was destined to play for the Boston Celtics.

At first Auerbach was disappointed because he thought Cousy was too short and too flashy. "Bob Cousy will have to make the team, just like anyone else," the coach declared.

It took Cousy a little while to prove himself. The young guard had trouble adjusting to Auerbach's disciplined style of play, and his Celtics teammates had trouble latching onto

Bob Cousy, the first Celtics star.

Dennis Johnson was another fine Boston guard.   11

Bill Sharman made 87 percent of his free-throw attempts to lead the NBA.

some of his razzle-dazzle passes. Gradually, however, everything came together, and Boston's two little giants—Red Auerbach and Bob Cousy—started a basketball dynasty.

Over the next 13 years—until he retired in 1963—Bob Cousy displayed skills that earned him the reputation as the best ball handler in the NBA. His behind-the-back dribbling and no-look passes revolutionized guard play in professional basketball. And he wasn't a bad scorer either, with an average of 18.5 points per game over his career.

"God handed out some great gifts to Bob Cousy," said Hall of Famer Bobby Wanzer. "He made him 6-foot-1 with a skinny body and powerful legs that can run all night. He gave him a poker face that never tips off his emotions. There are some nights when he just can't be stopped. No matter how closely you guard him, he's still going to score from all angles. He'll take shots no other player will attempt and make them."

"BIG BILL" PROVIDES THE MISSING INGREDIENT

During Bob Cousy's first six years directing the team (1951–56), Auerbach's Celtics recorded four second-place finishes in the NBA's Eastern Division. Other Boston stars of the period included two future Hall of Famers—a deadly accurate guard named Bill Sharman, one of the NBA's all-time great foul shooters, and a smooth, skinny center/forward named "Easy Ed" Macauley. But to be a championship contender the team still needed a big man who could dominate on the defensive end. Auerbach knew just who he wanted to fill this role, a 6-foot-9 center from the University of San Francisco named William Felton Russell.

"I'd heard about Russell when he was a sophomore at San Francisco," Auerbach said. "My old college coach, Bill Reinhart, saw him play. He told me, 'Red, you've got two years. Start planning now. This kid can be outstanding.'"

Auerbach knew he wanted Russell, but getting him was another matter. The Celtics didn't have one of the top draft picks in 1956, and Russell would certainly be taken before Boston's turn arrived. So Auerbach started wheeling and dealing, a skill he was famous for. He traded Macauley and a young star named Cliff Hagan to St. Louis for the second pick in the draft and used that pick to select Russell. Boston fans thought the coach was crazy. They wondered: Why trade an established star and crowd favorite like Macauley for an untried rookie?

Even Auerbach had doubts at first. "Did I know what I was getting? Not really. A great rebounder? Sure. But I knew nothing about his character, his smarts, his heart—things like that. You never know these things until you actually have the guy on your team. No one in the league really thought about it at the time. They certainly didn't know what was to happen—11 Boston championships in the next 13 years."

During his NBA career, Bill Russell profoundly changed professional basketball. He showed that a big man could control a game not by scoring, but with defense and rebounding. According to Auerbach, Russell could "play a whole team defensively. He could get anything within 15 feet of the basket, blocking as many as four separate shots

1 9 5 7

With a 16.2 average, Tom Heinsohn was the NBA's highest-scoring rookie.

on one play. Because of Bill Russell, defense became an important part of basketball."

In Russell's rookie year, 1956–57, the Celtics won their first NBA championship. Another first-year player, Tom Heinsohn, provided needed offense. A 6-foot-7 forward from Holy Cross, Heinsohn was named Rookie of the Year.

"We've been trying to get to the top for seven years and now we're finally here," hollered Bob Cousy during the locker room celebration. "People are calling us great, but now we have to do it again, to show we are the greatest."

Although the Celtics were edged out in the NBA finals the next season by the St. Louis Hawks, Boston was back on top in 1958–59. After adding three future Hall of Famers—Sam Jones, K.C. Jones, and Frank Ramsey—Boston rebounded to win its second world title in three years, this time over Elgin Baylor and the Minneapolis Lakers.

The Celtics dynasty was now established. In 1959–60, they became only the second team to win back-to-back NBA championships. But they weren't through yet. During the next six seasons, the basketball world sat spellbound as Auerbach turned Bill Russell and company loose on a record-setting rampage that resulted in eight consecutive titles—more than has been compiled by any other team in sports history. Now the Celtics were, indeed, "the greatest."

"MR. ENERGY"

Boston's overwhelming success was due in large part to Auerbach's ability to surround his big man—Bill Russell—with great role players who would concentrate on

1 9 5 8

Bill Russell gave a sign of things to come by grabbing 40 rebounds in a game against Cincinnati.

Future Hall of Famer Tom Heinsohn.

1 9 6 3

Bob Cousy ended his Celtics career with his 13th straight 1,000-point season.

scoring or ballhandling or defense. During the middle of the Celtics' dynasty, Auerbach added a player who could fill all three roles and who, over time, would come to personify "Celtic Pride." That player was John Havlicek.

Coach Auerbach knew he had something special the first day he watched his 1962 first-round draft choice practice with the Celtics regulars. The rookie was running the veterans into exhaustion. Some players could shoot more accurately, rebound better, run faster, or jump higher than "Hondo"—but no one could outwork, outlast, or out-hustle him.

In his rookie season, Havlicek came off the bench to play guard and forward. It was like inserting a tornado into the lineup. The New York Knicks' Dick Barnett once joked that Hondo must have three lungs because he could run harder and longer than anyone in the league. Havlicek would continue his hustling style of play for the Celtics for 16 seasons. He was truly one of the greatest players ever to wear the Celtics' kelly green.

Havlicek also figured prominently in one of the most famous games in Celtics history. The date was April 15, 1965. The event was the seventh game of the Eastern Division finals. The Celtics were playing their chief rivals, the Philadelphia 76ers, who were led by basketball's greatest scoring machine, Wilt Chamberlain. With two minutes left in the game, Boston led by seven. It looked certain they would reach the NBA finals again. Then Chamberlain scored six quick points to cut the lead to 110–109 with only five seconds to go. It was Bill Russell's job to bring the ball in under the 76ers' basket so that Boston could run out the clock. But his pass hit a wire holding up the basket and fell out of bounds. It was Philadelphia's ball.

Philadelphia guard Hal Greer lobbed the inbound pass toward a teammate, but then, out of nowhere, came Hondo Havlicek. Hondo leaped high and tipped the ball to Sam Jones to save the game for Boston. "Havlicek stole the ball! Havlicek stole the ball!" shouted Celtics radio announcer Johnny Most. Boston fans still savor that magic moment.

Sam Jones led the Celtics in scoring and made his fourth All-Star Game appearance.

THE CHANGING OF THE GUARD

Havlicek's fourth season as a Celtic, 1965–66, was a landmark for the team. Once again, the Celtics won the league title, their eighth straight. But a magnificent era was coming to an end. During the playoffs, Red Auerbach announced that he would resign as coach and become the team's general manager instead.

Boston fans knew that Auerbach wouldn't be an easy man to replace, but Bill Russell took the guesswork out of the decision. "If I can't play for you, I'd rather play for myself, if you'll let me have the job," Russell told Auerbach. Auerbach approved of the idea, and Russell became the team's player/coach.

The towering Celtic dynasty did not topple with Auerbach's resignation, but its foundation did weaken. The next year, the Celtics lost their NBA crown to Wilt Chamberlain and the 76ers. Russell felt disgraced. Prior to losing to the 76ers, Russell had hinted at retirement. But now that was out of the question. He could not—and would not—accept

The mighty Bill Russell (pages 18–19).

1 9 7 2

John Havlicek earned the first of five consecutive berths on the NBA's All-Defensive team.

being second best. During the next two seasons, Russell led the team as both player and coach to its tenth and eleventh championships.

Russell stepped down before the 1969–70 season, ending his 13-year career in Boston. He passed the reins of the club to his former teammate, Tom Heinsohn. Unfortunately, without Russell in the middle, Heinsohn's Celtics lacked the dominating force that had kept them on top. But general manager Red Auerbach had the answer. Behind the scenes, Auerbach had been locating fresh new talent to continue the Celtic legacy. Heading the list of newcomers was Dave Cowens, a redheaded center from Florida State University. In some ways, Cowens was an oversized version of John Havlicek. Always hustling and scrapping, Cowens was not fluid or graceful, but he was effective. "Dave may have been the most emotional Celtic of all time," said Auerbach. "He played with incredible intensity. It was almost as if you could see sparks in his eyes when he made up his mind to do something."

By the 1973–74 season, Auerbach and Heinsohn had successfully rebuilt the Celtics around Cowens. On the roster were such players as Havlicek, Don Chaney, Don Nelson, Paul Silas, and Jo Jo White. Together they rocketed to 56 victories in the regular season. Then they toppled the Milwaukee Bucks, led by Kareem Abdul-Jabbar, in seven games in the championship round of the playoffs, bringing a twelfth banner to Boston Garden.

Two years later, the same lineup brought another title to Boston. That championship series, pitting the Celtics against Phoenix, included perhaps the greatest playoff game in NBA history. The heart-stopping fifth game of the series went into three overtimes, the first two ending in game-saving, last-second shots—one by Havlicek and one by Phoenix's Garfield Heard. The game also featured an illegal time-out call and a near-fight between the Boston fans and the referee. It was one of the wildest "Garden parties" ever. And, as usual, it had a happy ending for the Celtics.

1 9 7 6

Paul Silas, a power on the offensive boards, helped Boston rank as the league's top rebounding team.

FLYING HIGH WITH BIRD

Following the 1975–76 championship season, the fortunes of the Celtics took a turn for the worse again. First Havlicek retired, and then Dave Cowens called it quits. The team needed to be rebuilt—and they needed a star to rebuild around.

Once again, Red Auerbach had a plan. During the first round of the 1978 college draft, he selected Larry Bird of Indiana State University, even though Bird still had a year of eligibility left at ISU. It was a big gamble. For Bird to become a Celtic, he would have to be signed before the 1979 draft was held; otherwise, another team could choose him. And because Bird knew how important he was to Auerbach and the Celtics, he demanded a lot of money before he would agree to play for Boston.

It became a battle of wills—and dollars. At first, Auerbach was unwilling to give in to Bird's demands. He felt that a dynasty could not be built around a forward. "No forward can do it by himself, because forwards are at the mercy of the center to get the ball and of the guards to pass it to them," he insisted. Still, Red knew that Larry Bird was a special,

21

The one and only Larry Bird.

proud, Celtic type of player. Luckily for Boston fans, the two men finally worked out a deal.

Auerbach has never regretted his decision—Bird has gone on to become, in the words of one NBA coach, "the most determined, tough-minded, and competitive player I have ever seen." Another opposing coach was asked how best to defend against Bird. "Pray he gets sick," was the reply.

Part of Bird's greatness was the effect his courage and drive had on his teammates. According to Celtics broadcaster Mike Gorman, "Larry forced others to play at a level of intensity that may not be natural for them—and he made them better players."

With Bird in the lineup for the 1979–80 season and new coach Bill Fitch at the helm, the Celtics compiled a 61–21 record, 32 wins better than the previous year—the greatest turnaround in NBA history. Bird was voted Rookie of the Year and named to the All-NBA team. But the Celtics failed to reach the finals that year, and neither Bird nor Auerbach was satisfied.

To help put the team on top again, Auerbach pulled off another one of his amazing deals. Boston had the first pick in the 1980 college draft. Auerbach traded his club's pick to the Golden State Warriors, who desperately wanted to choose a young center named Joe Barry Carroll. In exchange, Auerbach got Robert "the Chief" Parish, as well as the third pick in the draft, which he used to add 6-foot-10 rookie Kevin McHale to the Celts. In one brilliant move, Auerbach had brought to his team one of the fastest big men ever to play pro basketball (Parish) and an outstanding sixth man who could double as a power forward and center

1 9 8 0

Red Auerbach was named NBA Executive of the Year for his role in Boston's turnaround.

(McHale). Suddenly the Celtics became a bigger, quicker, and deeper team.

Nothing could stop them in 1980–81. They compiled a 62–20 record and then roared past the Chicago Bulls, Philadelphia 76ers, and Houston Rockets to win the club's first NBA crown since 1976.

1 9 8 1

Nate Archibald was voted the Most Valuable Player in the All-Star Game.

For Larry Bird, the win was special. "That's why I play," said Bird. "Winning the championship—I've never felt that way any other time, no matter how big some other game was. In the last game against Houston, we were way ahead at the end, and so I came out with three minutes left, and my heart was pounding so hard on the bench. I thought it would jump right out of my chest. You know what you feel? You just want everything to stop and stay that way forever."

The combination of Bird, Parish, McHale, and guards Dennis Johnson ("D.J.") and Danny Ainge powered the Celtics to the NBA finals four more times during the 1980s and brought home two more championship banners to Boston Garden in 1984 and 1986. But the club was slowly starting to age. The time had now come for Red Auerbach to begin rebuilding again.

PAINFULLY MOVING INTO THE 1990S

As Auerbach prepared for the 1986 college draft, he was looking forward to the challenge of bringing a youthful look back to the Celtics. He felt that the draft, in which Boston had the second pick overall, would set the stage for future Celtic championships in the 1990s. And he had just the player in mind to lead the kelly green into the next decade. The man he wanted was a 6-foot-8 forward from Maryland named Len Bias. Auerbach thought Bias had the tools to be a great player: speed, leaping ability, a good touch from the outside, and defensive intensity.

Unfortunately, pro basketball fans would never get to see Len Bias perform in Boston Garden. The night he was drafted by the Celtics, Bias went to a party to celebrate and fatally overdosed on drugs. The incident rocked the basketball world and shook up the Celtics. "There is no question that Len's death was a tragic loss to everyone and a sadness we will all carry with us," said Larry Bird.

Somehow the Celtics managed to hold things together during the 1986–87 season, but some of the heart was taken out of the team. They reached the NBA finals for a fourth straight year and an unprecedented 19th time, only to lose to the Los Angeles Lakers.

Red Auerbach and Boston management tried to rebound from the Bias loss with trades and draft picks that blended youth with the experience of the team's aging superstars. One of the best of these, forward Reggie Lewis—a picture-perfect jumper—was selected from Northeastern in the 1987 draft. He joined Larry Bird and Kevin McHale near the top of the league's scoring charts. "Lewis, with his multitude of weapons and ability to leap to the sky, will be a big-time scorer for a long time to come," said basketball analyst and former NBA great Rick Barry.

All-Star Kevin McHale shot .604 from the field to lead the NBA.

Scoring standout David Wesley (pages 26-27).

Reggie Lewis led Boston to 15 wins in its last 16 games and an Atlantic Division title.

The combination of aging veterans and young players with star potential continued to be the story of the Boston Celtics for the next several years. Through most of the early 1990s, the Celtics were still a playoff team, but were no longer one of the NBA's elite clubs. They were defeated in the playoffs by some of the league's new elite clubs, including the Cleveland Cavaliers and the Orlando Magic. The 6-foot-7 Lewis emerged as a team leader and a scoring machine, averaging over 20 points per game, but Bird found himself on the bench more and more with injuries—most notably an ailing back.

Bird stayed healthy long enough to play for the first U.S. Dream Team in the 1992 Summer Olympic Games in Barcelona, Spain. He retired from the Celtics shortly thereafter, however, because of recurrent back problems. In 13 seasons, Bird had won three NBA championships for the Celtics and had been voted the league's Most Valuable Player three times. He is remembered as a proud Celtic and also for his rivalry with the Lakers' Magic Johnson. It was Johnson's and Bird's rivalry that is credited for making the NBA as popular as it is today.

Without Bird, Lewis and aging teammates Parish and McHale still managed to make the playoffs in 1992–93. But in game one against the Charlotte Hornets, Lewis collapsed on the court. He was diagnosed with an irregular heartbeat, a condition called arrhythmia. Without Lewis, the Celtics lost to the Hornets in four games.

Then, while shooting baskets in the off-season at Brandeis

University, Lewis collapsed again. Paramedics found Lewis in complete cardiac arrest. They tried to revive him, but it was too late. Lewis, an NBA All-Star, died playing the game he loved. Two years later, he would be posthumously inducted into Northeastern's Sports Hall of Fame.

During that same off-season, McHale retired and Parish signed with the Charlotte Hornets. After all this, the team needed some change for the good. In 1995 the Celtics moved to a new arena, where they hoped to make a fresh start. All the old championship banners that had once decorated the Boston Garden now hung as inspiration to the team in their new home, the FleetCenter.

Hoping to add more banners to his team's collection, Coach M.L. Carr—a former Celtic player—nabbed the 1996 first-round draft choice, Antoine Walker. Coach Carr believed Walker was the perfect pick.

"This kid has special talents," Carr said. "He does a lot of things well. He shoots the ball well from the outside and has a nice post-up game. For his size, he handles the ball and passes it as well as anyone that we have had here since Larry Bird."

The 6-foot-8 Walker led his college team, the Kentucky Wildcats, to an NCAA championship as a sophomore, and then decided he was ready to be a pro.

"I haven't seen too many 6-foot-8 kids who can do the things that kid can do," said University of Utah coach Rick Majerus. "He handles the ball well. He shoots it. He takes it to the basket. He rebounds. He gets deflections. He throws alley-oops. He catches alley-oops."

"I know I'm not going to come in and be a high-impact

1 9 9 4

Native Croatian Dino Radja made the NBA All-Rookie second team.

The versatile Rick Fox.

Dee Brown, an unrelenting guard.   31

1 9 9 7

Brett Szabo felt the luck of the Irish on St. Patrick's Day, scoring 10 points, a career high.

player and score 30 points immediately," said Walker. "I'm just going to step in and help out as much as I can. I'm going to bring a winning attitude and hopefully I can bring more championships to Boston."

With Walker's steady development, the Celtics looked like a team on the rise. An off-season deal that sent Eric Montross to the Dallas Mavericks gave the Celtics the pick they needed to get Walker and another pick in a future draft. Carr believed the trade helped the Celtics turn the corner.

"I think that was a big step in the right direction in terms of a comeback," said Carr. "For our core players, like Eric Williams, Rick Fox, David Wesley, Dana Barros, and Dino Radja, it now gives us an opportunity to start to put some things together."

Corraling Antoine Walker was Carr's last great move for the Celtics. After the 1996–97 season, Carr stepped down from his coaching and administrative duties. The club then went after legendary Kentucky coach Rick Pitino, who, after several weeks of media speculation, accepted the top seat at Boston. Fans are excited about the change, and the players are hoping that it won't be long before they're filling the FleetCenter like they used to fill Boston Garden. The road ahead may be rough, but if Walker continues to improve, and if the club can add more quality players through free agency and the draft, Pitino's optimism and energy won't go to waste. Then perhaps the FleetCenter will be home to yet another banner displayed in the name of "Celtic Pride."